OUT OF → THIS WORLD

VIRGINIA LOH-HAGAN

ORIGINS
OF LIFE

45TH PARALLEL PRESS

Published in the United States of America
by Cherry Lake Publishing
Ann Arbor, Michigan
www.cherrylakepublishing.com

Reading Adviser: Marla Conn, MS, Ed.,
  Literacy specialist, Read-Ability, Inc.
Book Designer: Jessica Rogner

Photo Credits: © Color4260/Shutterstock, cover, 1; © NASA, ESA,
  and the Hubble Heritage Team (STScI/AURA)/NASA ID: GSFC_20171208_
  Archive_e001885, 5; © Tim Bertelink/WikiMedia, 7, 12; © Bulgac/
  iStock, 8; © Beate Wolter/Shutterstock, 11; © Dotted Yeti/Shutterstock,
  15; © Nicolas Primola/Shutterstock, 16; © Paleocolour/WikiMedia, 19;
  © Gerhard Boeggemann/WikiMedia, 21; Photo taken and uploaded by:
  Mohatatou/Wikimedia, 23; © MichaelTaylor3d/Shutterstock, 25; Contributed
  by MBLWHOI Library/Illustration by: John Gould/Public Domain, 27;
  Contributed by London Stereoscopic and Photographic Company/
  WikiMedia/Public Domain, 29
Graphic Element Credits: © Trigubova Irina/Shutterstock

45th Parallel Press is an imprint of
Cherry Lake Publishing Group

Library of Congress Cataloging-in-Publication Data
Names: Loh-Hagan, Virginia, author. | Loh-Hagan, Virginia.
  Out of this world.
Title: Origins of life / by Virginia Loh-Hagan.
Description: Ann Arbor, Michigan : Cherry Lake Publishing, 2020 |
  Series: Out of this world | Includes bibliographical references
  and index.
Identifiers: LCCN 2020006919 (print) | LCCN 2020006920 (ebook) |
  ISBN 9781534169265 (hardcover) | ISBN 9781534170940 (paperback) |
  ISBN 9781534172784 (pdf) | ISBN 9781534174627 (ebook)
Subjects: LCSH: Life–Origin–Juvenile literature. | Evolution
  (Biology)–Juvenile literature.
Classification: LCC QH325 .L727 2020 (print) | LCC QH325 (ebook) |
  DDC 576.8--dc23
LC record available at https://lccn.loc.gov/2020006919
LC ebook record available at https://lccn.loc.gov/2020006920

Printed in the United States of America | Corporate Graphics

4 . . . . **INTRODUCTION**
What Is the Universe?

6 . . . . **CHAPTER ONE**
What Happened After the "Big Bang"?

10 . . . . **CHAPTER TWO**
What Were the First Signs of Life?

14 . . . . **CHAPTER THREE**
What Happened During the Paleozoic Era?

18 . . . . **CHAPTER FOUR**
When Did Dinosaurs Roam the Earth?

22 . . . . **CHAPTER FIVE**
Who Were the First Humans?

26 . . . . **CHAPTER SIX**
Who First Studied Evolution?

30 . . . . **GLOSSARY**

31 . . . . **FAR-OUT FACTS / LEARN MORE**

32 . . . . **INDEX / ABOUT THE AUTHOR**

WHAT IS THE UNIVERSE?

The universe is huge. It's everything that exists. This includes planets, stars, and outer space. It includes living things on Earth.

The universe contains billions of galaxies. Galaxies are huge space collections. Galaxies are made up of billions of stars, gas, and dust. Galaxies include **solar** systems. Solar means sun. Earth is in the Milky Way galaxy. Galaxies spin in space. They spin very fast. There's a lot of space between stars and galaxies. This space is filled with dust, light, heat, and rays.

Before the birth of the universe, there was no time, space, or matter. Anything that takes up space is matter. Matter can exist in different states. The common states include solid, liquid, and gas. This is why things like air and smoke are considered matter. But the heat and light from a fire aren't matter. These don't take up space.

The universe hasn't always been the same size. It also hasn't always existed. Some scientists believe it began with a "big bang."

 The Milky Way galaxy is large. But there are other galaxies far larger than ours!

This is a **theory**. Theory means an idea. This theory explains how the universe was born. First, the universe was a super tiny blob, smaller than a pinhead! Then, that super tiny blob exploded. This happened 13.8 billion years ago. Next, energy spread out. Energy is made from matter. For example, the flames in a fire are matter. They take up space. But the heat you feel and the light you see from the flames are energy. Last, stars and planets formed. This all happened in less than a second.

Scientists think the universe is still expanding. Expanding means growing or spreading out. Scientists also think this expanding process is speeding up.

CHAPTER ONE

WHAT HAPPENED AFTER THE "BIG BANG"?

Evolution is the gradual change of life on Earth over time. Scientists find and study **fossils**. Fossils are traces of life-forms that lived a long time ago. They can be bones, shells, or other parts. These fossils can be found in certain rocks. What is known about life on Earth comes from studying these fossils. The **origins** of life can be explained by studying eras of Earth's history. Origin means beginning. An era is a period of time in history.

 The heat during this time melted rocks. No rocks from the Hadean Era survived.

The Hadean Era is the earliest part of Earth's history. It took place 4.5 billion years ago. It lasted about 700 million years. During this time, Earth was being formed.

After the big bang, there was space **debris**. Debris is the leftovers from crashes. Many objects were floating in space. These objects crashed into Earth. These impacts created volcanoes. Volcanoes are mountains. They have openings at the top. They blow up. They release hot gases and lava. Lava is hot melted rock.

There was no life at this time. It was too hot. Then, the Moon was formed. Oceans were formed. They were hot. But they cooled down. Earth went through extreme changes of hot and cold during the early period.

The Hadean Era was named after Hades. *Hades* is the ancient Greek word for "hell."

AMONG THE STARS: WOMEN IN SCIENCE

Dr. Sarah Blaffer Hrdy was born in 1946. She's a scientist. She taught at the University of California, Davis. She was selected as one of the top leaders in animal behavior. She is one of the most important women in science. She studies primate behavior. Primates include apes, monkeys, and humans. She studies human evolution. People thought human evolution was shaped by males. Males were thought to be in charge. Hrdy questioned this. She didn't think this was true. She went to India. She studied monkeys. She saw male monkeys killing their babies. She saw female monkeys work together. She saw the female monkeys fight off the males. This means females are strong. They're not the weaker sex. Hrdy wrote a book. The book is called *Mother Nature: A History of Mothers, Infants and Natural Selection*. It took her 15 years to write.

CHAPTER TWO

WHAT WERE THE FIRST SIGNS OF LIFE?

Signs of life appeared in the Archaean Era. The Archaean Era started about 3.8 billion years ago. Earth started to settle. Its crust cooled. Crust is the planet's top layer. It's the surface. Gases changed and formed. Solid rock formed. The first continents formed at this time. Continents are large areas of land.

There were **microbes**. Microbes are tiny organisms. They had one single cell. Cells are basic units of life. These microbes were so small. They couldn't be seen. They ate rock minerals. Their bodies were soft. They melted away when they died. They didn't leave behind any fossils.

The first fossils were from 3.5 billion years ago. Scientists had to use powerful **microscopes**. Microscopes are tools used to see very small things. These first fossils were part of groups of microbes. They're the first living things to get energy from sunlight.

 Early Archaean rocks can be found in Greenland, Canada, South Africa, and Western Australia.

The end of the Archaean Era saw more signs of life. There was no life on land. But there was life in the oceans. Soft-bodied creatures lived in the early oceans. This included jellyfish and worms. Earth was just starting to get oxygen. Oxygen is needed for life. It's needed for breathing.

 The Archaean Era is part of the Precambrian Period. This period is known as the Age of Early Life.

DOWN-TO-EARTH EXPERIMENT

Ever wondered how fossils are formed? Try out this experiment. Create your own "fossil." Think like a scientist!

Materials:

- Dried, used coffee grounds
- Salt
- Spoon
- Waxed paper
- Cup or glass
- Flour
- Bowl
- Cold coffee
- Small objects like shells, plants, or toys

Instructions:

1. Mix an equal amount of coffee grounds and flour. Add half the amount of salt in a bowl. (If you used 1 cup (236.6 milliliter) of coffee grounds and flour, add ½ cup (118.3 mL) of salt.) Mix the ingredients with a spoon.

2. Stir in half the amount of cold coffee. (If you used 1 cup (236.6 mL) of coffee grounds, stir in ½ cup (118.3 mL) of cold coffee.) You've made dough. This represents Earth's soil.

3. Press the dough onto the waxed paper. Shape the dough into a circle. You can use the opening of a cup or glass.

4. Press objects into the dough. Carefully lift them out. You've made a print. This represents a fossilized print.

5. Let the dough prints harden overnight. When the clay hardens, the print will still be there.

Animal and plant prints turn into fossils. They're pressed into rock just like the prints you made in this activity.

CHAPTER → THREE

WHAT HAPPENED DURING THE PALEOZOIC ERA?

The Paleozoic Era began 542 million years ago. There were many changes. Life with multiple cells developed. This era became the "time of fishes." The oceans became full of life. Corals formed. They provided homes to sea animals. Animals with hard bodies formed. Clams and snails formed. The first **vertebrates** formed. Vertebrates are animals with skeletons inside their bodies. These vertebrates were fish-like animals. But they didn't have jaws.

Plants were the first life on land. This happened 420 million years ago. Early plants looked like moss. Later, ferns and the first trees formed.

 Many fossils of strange-looking creatures were found from this era.

Some early fish had lungs and gills. They moved from the oceans. They moved into shallow waters. Then, they moved onto land. **Tetrapods** were the first land animals. Tetrapods are vertebrates with 4 legs. Reptiles and amphibians formed. This happened around 360 million years ago. Early animals included lizards, snakes, and crocodiles.

Insects formed. Early insects were big. Spiders and dragonflies were some of the first insects. Cockroaches also formed. They were found all over Earth.

This era ended with a huge mass **extinction**. Extinction means dying out. This happened 245 million years ago. About 90 to 95 percent of life was wiped out. But this allowed new animals to form.

Reasons for the extinction include climate change or a comet crash. Climates are weather conditions.

IT'S (ALMOST) ROCKET SCIENCE

Paleontologists are dinosaur scientists. They're like Earth astronauts. They don't travel to space. Instead, they "travel" back in time. They help reveal the mysteries of Earth's past. They discover and study fossils. They use a lot of tools. They use electron microscopes. These microscopes can focus really well. They can see the smallest details of the smallest fossils. They can see tissues. They can see cells. Paleontologists also use CT scanners. These tools let paleontologists see inside fossils. They have x-ray tubes. These tubes rotate around fossils. They shoot out skinny, powerful x-rays. These x-rays can get through solid materials like rocks. They're dangerous. They'd do great damage to humans. Digital detectors pick up signals from the x-rays. Then, paleontologists use computer programs. These programs analyze the signals. They turn signals into different images. They put these images together. They rebuild models of the dinosaur skeletons. They make three-dimensional (3D) models. 3D means looking real, not flat. 3D models have height, width, and depth. This way, we can see what dinosaurs really looked like.

CHAPTER FOUR

WHEN DID DINOSAURS ROAM THE EARTH?

After the extinction came the Mesozoic Era. It started around 252 to 245 million years ago. During the previous era, the early continents had formed into **Pangaea**. Pangaea is all of the continents merged as one. During the Mesozoic Era, the continents broke apart. Shallow seas spread out. Mountains formed. The weather was hot and humid. Lands were covered with green plants. These plants were a great food source.

The African T. rex was one of the last dinosaurs alive before extinction.

This era is known as the "age of the dinosaurs." Dinosaurs spread out. They took over the land. They took over the seas. They were all over Earth. Like all early animals, they laid eggs.

Dinosaurs were **herbivores** or **carnivores**. Herbivores eat plants. Carnivores eat meat. Dinosaurs were on Earth for 180 million years.

Some scientists think a space object crashed into Earth. Some think volcanoes erupted. Either way, the Sun was blocked. Plants stopped growing. Herbivores were the first to die. Then, carnivores died. Dinosaurs became extinct. Only dinosaurs that evolved into flightless birds survived. This happened 65 million years ago.

Small mammals formed at this time. Mammals are warm-blooded animals. They have hair or fur. They feed milk to their young. They give live births. The first mammal looked like a small mouse. Mammals lived with dinosaurs. But dinosaurs ate them. When dinosaurs went extinct, the remaining animals thrived.

 The Mesozoic Era has 3 time periods: Triassic, Jurassic, and Cretaceous.

CHAPTER → FIVE

WHO WERE THE FIRST HUMANS?

The period we are currently in is the Cenozoic Era. It began 65 million years ago. Continents formed in their current locations. Continents are now spread far apart. Each continent had different climates. Animals and plants spread out. They evolved. They **adapted** to their climates. Adapted means to make changes.

At first, there were lots of forests. There was an ice age. Earth became cool and dry. This created more open lands. It created more grasslands. Flowering plants grew all over. This meant more food. Mammals became the dominant **species**. Species are animal groups. All species evolved into their present-day forms during this era.

Without dinosaurs, large flightless birds became **predators**.
Predators are hunters. These birds are called "terror birds."
More animals formed. Cave bears, saber-toothed cats, and
woolly mammoths roamed the earth. Oceans widened,
and sharks and whales thrived.

 We're still living in the Cenozoic Era.

The first primates formed. Early primates looked like squirrels with monkey hands. They had thumbs to grasp things. Early primates formed around 60 million years ago.

The first **hominids** formed about 6 million years ago. Hominids are early human-like mammals. They didn't look like humans today. According to scientists, there were several different types of human species, like Neanderthals and Homo sapiens. Homo sapiens were the only surviving species. Homo sapiens are modern humans. They formed about 100,000 years ago. They became predators. Many animals went extinct.

 Several ice ages happened during this era. This forced life to grow around the equator.

CHAPTER → SIX

WHO FIRST STUDIED EVOLUTION?

Charles Lyell lived from 1797 to 1875. He was a Scottish **geologist**. Geology is the study of Earth's history as recorded in rocks. Lyell wanted to prove that Earth was formed from natural events. He said that Earth's crust formed from small changes. These small changes took place over time. Lyell also said that Earth was very old. His ideas changed people's thinking.

Charles Darwin was inspired by Lyell. Darwin said species changed over time. He lived from 1809 to 1882. He was British. He studied nature and life sciences. He's best known for his theory of evolution.

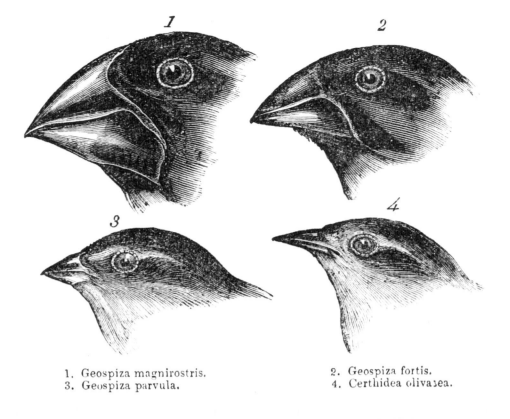

1. Geospiza magnirostris.
3. Geospiza parvula.

2. Geospiza fortis.
4. Certhidea olivasea.

 Darwin and Lyell were radical thinkers for their time.

Darwin traveled around the world. He studied plants. He studied birds. He studied fossils. In 1859, he wrote *On the Origin of Species*. Darwin said species survived by adapting or evolving. Species evolved by changing to fit their environments. Darwin believed the species we know today had evolved from common **ancestors**. Ancestors are early plants or animals.

Alfred Russel Wallace lived from 1823 to 1913. He also studied nature and life sciences. He also came up with the theory of evolution. He did this separately from Darwin. But Darwin got all the credit. Like Darwin, Wallace traveled to do his studies. He was an expert on **biogeography**. Biogeography is the study of plants and animals in different climates.

Wallace and Darwin shared the same theory of evolution.

29

ADAPTED (uh-DAPT-id) changed as needed

ANCESTORS (AN-ses-turz) plants or animals that came before current ones

BIOGEOGRAPHY (bye-oh-jee-AH-gruh-fee) the study of plants and animals in different geographic areas

CARNIVORES (KAHR-nuh-vorz) meat eaters

DEBRIS (duh-BREE) leftover pieces from a crash

EXTINCTION (ik-STINGKT-shuhn) process of dying out or being wiped out

FOSSILS (FAH-suhlz) traces of life-forms that lived a long time ago

GEOLOGIST (jee-AH-luh-jist) person who studies Earth's history as recorded in rocks

HERBIVORES (HUR-bih-vorz) plant eaters

HOMINIDS (HAHM-ih-nidz) early animals that looked like humans

MICROBES (MYE-krobez) tiny organisms

MICROSCOPES (MYE-kruh-skopes) tools used to see very small things

ORIGINS (OR-ih-jinz) beginnings

PANGAEA (pan-JEE-uh) all of the continents merged as one big continent

PREDATORS (PRED-uh-turz) hunters

SOLAR (SOH-lur) relating to the sun

SPECIES (SPEE-sheez) animal groups

TETRAPODS (TEH-truh-pahdz) vertebrates with four legs

THEORY (THEER-ee) an idea meant to explain something

VERTEBRATES (VUR-tuh-brits) animals with skeletons inside their bodies

FAR-OUT FACTS

- There are different theories about the origins of life. One theory is panspermia. Panspermia states that life didn't begin on Earth. Life was brought from space. Space objects crashed into each other. Rocks from these crashes landed on Earth. These rocks had microbes. These microbes started life. This would mean that we're alien life-forms!

- Archaeopteryx is the earliest known bird. Its fossil was found in 1861. It was found in Germany. The animal is a stage between dinosaurs and birds. It has feathers. It has a long, bony tail. It's about the size of a raven. It's the first proof of Darwin's theory of evolution.

- Many animals can move their ears. They do this to hear sounds better. About 10 to 20 percent of humans can wriggle their ears. Most humans cannot. They don't need to. They don't need to hunt. They're not hunted. They lost this ability when they started to live in groups.

LEARN MORE

Claybourne, Anna, and Wesley Robins (illustr.). *Amazing Evolution: The Journey of Life.* London: Ivy Kids, 2019.

Jenkins, Martin, and Grahame Baker-Smith (illustr.). *Life: The First Four Billion Years: The Story of Life from the Big Bang to the Evolution of Humans.* Somerville, MA: Candlewick Studio, 2019.

INDEX

animals, 15, 22, 23
Archaean Era, 10, 11–12

"big bang," 4–5, 6–9

Cenozoic Era, 22, 23
continents, 10, 18, 22
Cretaceous period, 20
crust, earth's, 10, 26

Darwin, Charles, 26–27, 28, 31
dinosaurs, 17, 18–21

Earth, 4, 6, 7, 8, 10, 12, 16, 19, 20, 22
evolution, 6, 9, 22, 26–29, 31
experiment, 13
extinction, mass, 16, 18, 20, 23

fish, 14, 15
fossils, 6, 10–11, 13, 15, 17, 31

Hadean Era, 7, 8
hominids, 24
Homo sapiens, 24
Hrdy, Sarah Blaffer, 9
humans, first, 22–25

ice age, 22, 24

Jurassic period, 20

life, first signs of, 6, 10–13, 31
Lyell, Charles, 26

mammals, 20
matter, 4, 5
Mesozoic Era, 18
microbes, 10, 11, 31

Neanderthals, 24

oceans, 8, 12, 14
origins of life, 6, 10–13, 31
oxygen, 12, 16

Paleozoic Era, 14–17
Pangaea, 18
panspermia, 31
plants, 14, 18, 22
predators, 23
primates, 24

space debris, 8

tetrapods, 15
Triassic period, 20

universe, 4–5

vertebrates, 14, 15
volcanoes, 8, 20

Wallace, Alfred Russel, 28
women, 9

ABOUT THE AUTHOR

Dr. Virginia Loh-Hagan is an author, university professor, and former classroom teacher. She is totally crazy about dinosaurs! She lives in San Diego, California, with her very tall husband and very naughty dogs. To learn more about her, visit www.virginialoh.com.